# The Missing

# THE MISSING

POEMS

RANGI MCNEIL

THE SHEEP MEADOW PRESS
RIVERDALE-ON-HUDSON, NEW YORK

All inquiries and permission requests should be addressed to:
The Sheep Meadow Press
P.O. Box 1345
Riverdale-on-Hudson, New York 10471

Distributed by the University Press of New England.
Cover: Jennifer Loebsack, *Madison, Wisconsin, 1999.*
Designed and typeset by S.M.

Printed on acid-free paper in the United States. This book meets the guidelines for permanence and durability of the Committee on Production Guidelines for Book Longevity of the Council on Library Resources.

Library of Congress Cataloguing-in-Publication Data

McNeil, Rangi, 1974-
The missing : poems / Rangi McNeil
p. cm.
ISNBN 1-931357-09-9 (alk. paper)
I. Title.

PS3613.C586 M5 2003
811'.6--dc21

2002032755

We are grateful to the New York State Council on the Arts, a state agency, for their support.

The Sheep Meadow Press gratefully acknowledges a grant from the National Endowment for the Arts.

This book would not have been possible without the myriad friends who have helped to sustain me. And while I can not list them all by name a list is still required: Eric Brey, Bill Duncan, Philippa Angelides, Nicola Springer, Gina Sheh, Alexei Angelides, Aline Cautis, Stella Flores, Tama Tochihara, Ginny Martin, Iris Hernandez, Al Spuler, Patrick Masterson, Ryan Murphy, Sarah Mooney, Emily Clark, Douglas Browne, Alexander Heminway, Anna Delmoro-Peterson, April Stolz, Robin Beth Schaer, Keesha Wallace, Amir Brown, Jennifer Geran, Pedro Yanez, Alicia Powers, Jen Loebsack, Joseph Doyle Hankins, Vancisk Hanjaka, Sixto Wagan, Sam Jones, Loris Bradley, Monica Ferrell, Gaby Calvorcoressi, Tim Schwarzer, Christy Lohr, Dan Schwankl, David Parke, Alexander Heim and Kotcrczo Robert.

I am grateful to: Lucie Brock-Broido and Richard Howard for their attentions and dissimilar examples of brilliance; my aunts for a haphazard yet bountiful affection.

And to Carla Peterson for everything.

To the memory of my mother

For Kim, T.J., Tommy George
and Mrs. Margaret Stewart

## CONTENTS

## A NOTE ON RANGI MCNEIL'S *THE MISSING*

At Hadrian's hellenophile court in the second century A.D., a poetaster named Straton compiled an anthology of short poems dating from the dawn of Greek lyric poetry down to its final florescence. The Greek Anthology survived two Byzantine recensions to end up in a single manuscript in the library of the Count Palatine in Heidelberg—hence its alternative title, the Palatine Anthology. The twelfth book of this collection (recently and salaciously redeemed for English by Daryl Hine in the Lockert Library of Poetry in Translation) carries the subtitle *Musa Paidika* and consists of 258 epigrams on various aspects of pederasty; some of these are by the greatest poets of the Greek language, others by less well-known writers, and many are anonymous. Their tone ranges from funny and bawdy to grave and resigned, and the overall effect is one of witty longing and regret rather than satisfaction (Sappho). By the time this scabrous anthology was in proper hands, Roman poets from Catullus to Propertius, from Martial to Hadrian himself had produced an analogous corpus of epigrammatic verse in Latin, and for three or four "modern" centuries, from the Elizabethans to the late Augustans, English poets relished producing an equivalent series of versions which were more frequently the result of gentlemanly diversion than classical constraint.

An analogous note is occasionally struck in the casual poems of Thoreau (one of the few men in Concord who could read Greek), but, until Ezra Pound, the resonance of the Latin classical epigram and erotic elegy was not decisively heard in American poetry. All the more surprising, then, or perhaps not surprising at all, that these fifty close-set poems by a very young black man from North Carolina, who turned up at Columbia University's School of the Arts with his erotic jingles tintinabulating to the max, his attitudes sharpened to the danger point, should be the proper (i.e. provocative) modern texts to refresh the terms of this antique convention, and to remind us that no conventions—after all, what are they but a coming-together?—will be lost if the circumstances are right, the talents ready, the eyes and ears alert.

All of which conditions are met by McNeil in these narrow, close, tight, hard poems, which to call epigrams is merely a chip off the old marble. Their power is in their diversity, the notes struck are never the same tune. There are, of course, some constants in affective response: the subject, as we used to say, might well be the poet's missing mother:

> Another autumn of waiting
> for the sky to clear of an old sorrow
>
> The stars are dead
> that shimmer their elaborate reckoning
>
> Mother is gone
>
> And not to China, or Pittsburgh, or Barneys
> or heaven (though that would be quaint).
>
> I'm 27, right-handed, thin & no one's.

or farther on, his missing relatives:

> A story is told in the family
> that my first intelligible word
> was *rangi*
>
> I spoke it into the full-length mirrors
> lining the walls of grandmother's closet
> while my aunts

dressed for another family reunion
in the mosquito-moist air of July.

This morning in my bathroom mirror,
my head covered in shaving cream,
dots of blood,

I saw the now-dour aunts again, unruined
& half-naked, sharing cigarettes
& whiskey: they were vibrant girls

*fast* but discreet.

his missing lovers (I cannot keep quoting the apposite poems or I shall simply repeat the entire book in this introductory note), his missing landscapes, missing cities, missing friends, and missing past (well, one more, irresistible to comment):

Though a man & a lover of men
I know little of the men I come from.
I divine their voices, all past tense & departure
from women little known (so haphazard their love)
like reading erased sums in dime-store ledgers.
I add each column, carry the balance
in search of whole numbers—*perhaps* and *if only*
too readily reduced to be real denominators.

Some skills are not bettered by practice,
some equations dissolve in solving,
some men are at their best when leaving.

One soon sees that McNeil's true Penelope, to tweak Pound's famous line, is enjambment, and almost as soon one realizes why the book has the title it flaunts. However, what is not missing, ever, from these poems is heartbreak, and for erotic epigrams that stops a great many gaps. I'm happy to commend to readers of this new poet these bitter little pills disguised as one damn irritant after another; they will not dissolve on your tongue, but they will become part of your protection, if you want such a thing, against despair.

Richard Howard

# one

## POSTHUMOUS

The thickness of mud
against bare feet,

fresh-falling rain
into an open mouth,

the sound of his name
spoken often & in earnest –

ordinary, low-grade gifts. She was
his mother, she knew no miracles.

And between grief & nothing
she left him grief.

two

## WHAT BECOMES A LEGEND MOST
BORNE

This is what I want: a sharp sweet bullet
to the back of the head.

The body blood-free, for once quiet
& so attractively still.

No more pliant excuses
the truth: concrete, posthumous.

## MEN

Though a man & a lover of men
I know little of the men I come from.
I divine their voices, all past tense & departure
from women little known (so haphazard their love)
like reading erased sums in dime-store ledgers.
I add each column, carry the balance
in search of whole numbers—*perhaps* & *if only*
too readily reduced to be real denominators.

Some skills are not bettered by practice,
some equations dissolve in solving,
some men are at their best when leaving.

## FOR A SPARROW-LIMBED WOMAN

She had lost patience and perhaps
this dying was like that time baby
cottonmouths appeared
under the rotting woodpile
behind our house—startling, then not.

## EMERSONIAN

Tonight the night is circus-sized, the street
below my window post-shootout-quiet.

I love you to the grave, my corrosive
friend. I dream for you a hard salvation

and prepare for your absence: a winnowing we cannot
name, our tongues being the plebeians they are.

Given these days we must make of them
an accord: antibodies of resilience.

(Ignorance is not an explanation, pain
no proper excuse.) Remember me,

when you go, as a passion. I will stay on,
perfecting the art of standing aside.

## **WHAT BECOMES A LEGEND MOST**
CURRICULUM VITAE

Perhaps I was under-qualified for childhood
missing the workshop on foot-looseness & fancy-freedom
the seminar in experimentation

Perhaps some of us are born endangered
the last in our lines smitten with drain-cleaner
cocktails, convalescence & wonder

(How much do I owe my long-fecund sickness)
Perhaps I wouldn't change a thing

## DRY MAGIC

A pair of novices, we owed a lot
to anonymous tips:

*Harlem's hot tonight, lilac's the new black,*
*all bets are off.*

Our requisite white rabbits
were pulled alive from hats & cakes

& closets. Our swords swallowed,
torsos halved—bloodshed minimal.

## COLORED

It was summer, grandmother
& I shopping for boy's underwear
in an old local department store,
she in her favorite dress, ember-red,
short sleeved, its v-neck
highlighting her strong delicate shoulders,
her straight gray hair
sliding down her straight back.

Moving toward the cashier,
jockeys in hand, I suddenly
remembered the store's
four bathrooms.
Two in the front, to the left
of house wares, another pair
in the rear, just this side
of the padlocked storeroom door.

## EXHAUST

Only on freeways, and at night, do I believe
in love: taillights, turn signals, exit lanes.

But I'm no driver. Or navigator.
(I've been known to unravel).

The night he shot himself, my father wasn't interested in dinner.
I sat in the kitchen, with my cigarettes, listening.

## MUCH IS REQUIRED

Life is long & disadvantageously personal:
dogshit on shoes, cocks caught

in zippers, brittle bones, fever.
And in between, dreams.

I've come late to the beauties of black men,
but have always been enamored of the dead.

## A BRIEF HISTORY OF LOSS

In this mildewed shoebox, one photograph: by her girls
herded as it were, my grandmother amidst her daughters:
Rita, Evelyn, Phyllis, Diane, Karen, Maxine & Jean.

Each woman in full possession of her inheritance;
butter-thick voice, hair without kinks, skin preciously light
& a neatly tethered spirit.

(The background velveteen & undulant,
magenta, perhaps, or a more acidic hue.)
In this world parceling out would not do;

no fiefdom in the cold north hills would suffice
for everyone (the only option). Like successful
monarchs, the sisters learned to hold enemies close;

having decorated the same womb, shared bobby-pins
& synchronized periods, they were most intimate.
How still they sit, how resolute, how *almost*-true.

## CASSANDRA COMPLEX

Half-hard & wide awake, I hear
drug dealers on the corner,

old water inside the new radiator,
upstairs-neighbor in his *cha-cha* heels.

And what I know will do no good.

## ELEGY FOR MY FATHER

I have never liked cats for the startling violence
of a scratch, mid-purr.

And think it best that I take this stiff-necked manx
that spits & sprays & so resembles you,

into the backyard along with my shovel (shiny
as your pistol) & speak my peace there.

Afterwards, I will dig him a deep, square grave
and it will go unmarked.

## EPYLLION

For weeks we survived on an unsteady
diet of carols, clementines & peppermint

candy-canes. And a distance
which grew as gradually as our hair.

## **WHAT BECOMES A LEGEND MOST** ELECTION

Children will believe in anything
unicorns, say, or parricide.

Bush beat Dukakis (from January
well through October I'd dreamed

of inflation: black-booted dollar
signs, shallow mass-graves, so many

dark-ending streets) and mother
was everything: my spindly

shoelaces, the curl
of hair binding my cock,

the spittle smothering my lips.
We had no Switzerland, no mediator,

no truce. So I wished her away.
I simply wished her *away*.

## THIRSTY SEASON OF WAITING

Monica's bound for San Francisco, Keesha for Kingston.
Benjamin's back from Boulder, but only until Sunday.

Tumi's taken the veil; Eric a wife.
And I'm on 6th Avenue, at Waverly Place, with my hand

in the air, trying to hail a cab big enough to hold
my overnight bag, my books & my bruise.

## OUR MERIT IS IN THE VALUE OF THAT WHICH WE PUT AT HAZARD

for Alexander Heim

This afternoon in the Pittsburgh International Airport
        I came this () close to buying a tiny, eat-your-heart-out

red bikini, a can of salted cashew nuts
        & a gun. (Nothing special,

just enough heat to keep the world
        honest & at bay.)

three

## IN THE COUNTRY OF MOTHERS

She said *look. This is a knife.*
*It's sharp & not to be trusted.*

And closed her palm around
the silver serrated blade: blood-red

blood beaded in the kitchen sink.

## APPENDAGE

The cute middle-aged poet flinched when I said:
*his pistol & really good aim*

in answer to his: *how did your father die?*
I've never been good at picking up guys or telling the truth.

My blonde roommate waits tables at French Roast
some nights I flirt with her manager, he likes

*skinny boys with big dicks—*
but it's my tongue that's wily, priceless.

## THE AUNTS SPEAK OF RESTRAINT

Ours is the lair of prudent over possible: reflex of silence.
If inanimate we'd be handcuffs: shiny metal precise.

## A BOY

Perhaps it would have been more helpful, more
informative, had the maternity nurse written
*contents under pressure* instead of *R. McNeil, boy*
on my blue newborn's bracelet.

It could have made all the difference, saved us trouble
down the road. If nothing more it could have given mother
pause to think this one thing through (of course
this is all speculation).

In the end, I went home marked like other boys
of my generation, took to feeding & lullabies
with average enthusiasm. I did not cry too much
nor speak too early.

But how many times mother found me in the crib staring—
mouth agape, limbs jackknifed & irregular.
No amount of calling could change my condition.
And no doctor could name it.

# CORRESPONDENCES

For every season there is a mythology
a story best told in pieces—
this is winter's:
coldness like leave-taking,
goose-feather overcoats lined with secrets.

## THE BED SHARED. THE PILLOW NOT.

I'm glad that Spain was refreshing,
that the new boy is a doll.

In the photos you could be brothers,
your true age doesn't show through.

Here, just above sea level, summer
festers like sweat in sour crotches.

And sometimes, when the wind is right,
I regret nothing.

## THE TALKING CURE

I did not think it worth my while
to fall in love

with an old man.
To push up against

a wintered chest.
To bind my hand

to his early mornings
& easy evenings.

I rely too deeply on night,
the white-powdered

belly-crawl against quiet,
whiskey & its whiteout.

Some doors need locks
& locking:

Behind them the leather sofa,
not exactly for sitting.

I do not think it worth my while.
Not now, not yet.

## TO THE MOTHER FROM A DISTANCE OF SOME YEARS

My days are like long division.
My best nights, Catholic-schoolgirl-dirty.

## TRANSATLANTIC

Tim calls from Bremen: he's left
his girlfriend and needs a place to crash.

He's tall & blonde & frequents public toilets.
We've been friends since 1992.

(Years ago, I overdosed instead of visiting him
at Christmas.  He waited in the Hamburg airport

for fourteen hours. His parents haven't forgiven me.)
I wonder how long he'll last.

## MY SWEET CAROLINA

I underestimated the heat. Forgot that it liquefies lips & limbs;
that the sun doesn't shine so much as strike, a broad-day
vigilante; that, in these houses, there's never shade sufficient.

Between us (1,191 days later) it's still
the playground at recess: dirty words, amateur intrigues,
the reckless bravado of the unchaperoned.

The 4-lane blacktop leading out of town still incomplete;
the 1-room public library in no need of addition;
Main Street empty; Patterson Cemetery green & eager.

We are our best in photographs; red-eyed & underexposed:
we lack the dimensions to harm. Yet standing shoulder
to shoulder we could be a matchbook waiting to spark.

## THE SURVIVING SISTERS CONSIDER

Evelyn died and we were the same (only less):
        a hot-rod, absent power steering.

## NEIGHBORS

Mr. Rufus & Mrs. Josephine are dead. He went first,
perhaps uninterested in one-sided arguments, she soon followed.
Their granddaughter kept the house. She's fine despite recent
break-ins.

(Plenty of stars, though fireflies
are scarce and the back-porch railing won't support my weight)

Cousin Preston's engaged and the boy from junior high,
the one with the appendectomy scar & real soft mouth,
killed a man during a game of spades.

(At night the city sprays for mosquitoes; it's hard
to pick up honeysuckle scent)

Mrs. Estelle says I talk like a white man
must be the schooling & traveling: *Yes ma'am.*
*I'm a pretty hard dog to keep on the porch.*

# NEXT AND LAST STOP

I've been on the road for sixteen days: Providence,
East Lansing, Salt Lake City, Raleigh, Memphis, Seattle.
Airports, freeways, Greyhound.

My sinuses are clogged;
I hate my suitcase.
And have my doubts about America.

## HOUSTON

I took his last white wife-beater,
a blue Hanukkah lamp, a length of gray rope.
The white for summer, blue for luck

& gray just in case.
I moved into the building opposite.
My kitchen faced his bathroom:

cooking & shitting synched.
He joined a gym. I bleached my eyebrows.
We rarely met on the street.

## ALMOST AUGUST

and unlike this time last year, it's not too hot to be alive.
        Days are dim & industrious,
nights I watch porn filmed in your country

        (pork-fed boys with just enough Hollywood glaze
to suggest delight) as if it were a travel program.
        I almost overlook the pert asses & cocks

hungering for a different view: the opera house,
        the car I totaled, the bride you left. I turn up the volume,
straining to hear some of the language the fucking muffles.

## IN TRUTH

I meant to say this city is always big
and I am not;

(noise in the evening,
in sunshine & —)

rather, words wince & falter
inside my throat

like albino eyes
under bright tight lights.

## THE THEME OF EFFORT PERSISTS

2:15 a.m. I'm now twenty-six. Another year
in my mouth & out my ass
and what?

The blood tests confirm: I've got two
narrow feet deep in the clause between dying
& living as well as I should.

Still I'm too young to use
*worthless, empty, wasted*
with any real conviction.

## WHAT MASTERY LIES IN LEAVING

for Alexander Alva Heminway

Often I've lingered under a strange roof, wet with rain,
thinking of home & its consequence;

my little hood with many bells jangling:
my trust & tether.

It rarely rains in Manhattan.
None of us is native here—

The Hudson a gray, sluggish river.

## NUMINOUS

For three days running, a pod of pilot whales
has beached itself along Cape Cod.

Some succumb to the sun, those that survive are relaunched
only to return, the following morning, a little farther up the coast.

Despair is a simple thing
like lighting, quicksand, or despair.

## FEW ARE CHOSEN

(Douglas has given himself over to the piano. Daily-lessons
on the Steinway in his rectangular living room. And Carla continues to
espouse *Revolution*.)

Sunday 5:45 a.m. a still-young man & his borrowed
doberman, liege & liege in this city that sleeps in shifts.
He awaits his calling, a calling profound in its specificity,
and traps rain water in a metal sieve—salvation in impending drought.

(Alexander is moving to Mexico to write without the worries of work.
Robin has her husband, students, mother, father, brothers & faith.)

## METAPHOR

I could love, but never live with, a three-legged dog
haven't the stamina for hip-hopping

down sidewalks or wobbly curb crossings.
I can forego the dignities of disability—

give me the right,
the regular.

## IN THE AFTERLIFE

For Emily a hammer & a bottle of champagne.
Poppy pretends not to comprehend but inches closer

to the gilt-frame mirror.
Sarah wants the coarse, the fretted.

Chris at least one of everything, two if illicit.
The tall patent attorney requests

three-day work weeks, foreign films,
a double-headed dildo;

his waiter-date, though, a helping of absolute darkness,
a side of peace & quiet.

## AGAINST MAGIC

A man in London loves me.
I don't know his name, but he's tall & sly.

The Supreme Court has ruled that fingerprints,
as evidence, are no longer infallible.

(I'll continue to burn my nail clippings
to prevent collection & bewitching.)

## VIBRATIONS IN THE GROUND

After predators, falling trees are the leading
cause of death among beavers.

Under stress, modern reptiles (crocodiles, say,
or Komodo dragons) tend to eat their young.

A pound of eyelashes & a pound of poison weigh the same—
your wet breath against my chest will not forestall an end.

## APPRENTICE

The Laotian student-barber speaks
too little English to shoot the shit

he's a total fuck-up, rarely
cleans his nails & is, by far, my favorite

(as of yesterday it's irrevocably fall;
the future cozy as concrete)

and I wonder what's Laotian for: *this isn't what I wanted;*
*I can't go out like this.*

## BACK OUT OF ALL THIS NOW TOO MUCH FOR US

If this were a movie instead of Tuesday night at my place
there'd be a disembodied voice to insure narrative cohesion:

the brunette by the refrigerator is a friend from college.
She has a thing for pork rinds, dirty martinis & wives.

The redhead in the hall is Joe.
I loved him without precision.

The music is *Nina Simone Live*, a double CD of performances
recorded between 1968 & 1972. I prefer the second disc.

My beard is eight days old
and is loosely based upon an emotion.

## IN A MANNER MUCH LIKE FORGETTING

There's no doubt that had I fallen during a getaway
he would have left me bleeding

& empty-handed on the sidewalk or shoulder
to reap our just deserts.

He would not have slowed or paused
to blow my brains out, mercifully.

True love has two colors: red & not-red.

four

## LAST NIGHT IN TEXAS

In a back bedroom, the window
facing the garden that did not

survive the summer,
during a party thrown in my honor,

he steps, again, into his jeans
& says I'm tough;

not cowboy movie star tough,
but like walking-feet, long

unaccustomed to shoes. *I think*
*they call that calloused*, I say.

He says, *they do.*

## RETROGRADE

Mid-summer & just after lunch.
My powder-blue bikini taut

across his ass, hands empty,
eyes hooded: asleep.

*It gets late early lately.*

We are sick of trying:
the laundry & weather too much

& also the ground.
Waves, this far south, are pathological.

We take our chances with riptide,
jellyfish, exhaustion.

## TIME AND RUINATION

A story is told in the family
that my first intelligible word
was *rangi.*

I spoke it into the full-length mirrors
lining the walls of grandmother's closet
while my aunts

dressed for another family reunion
in the mosquito-moist air of July.

This morning in the bathroom mirror,
my head covered in shaving cream,
dots of blood,

I saw the now-dour aunts again, unruined
& half-naked, sharing cigarettes
& whiskey: they were vibrant girls

*fast* but discreet.

## THIS MORTAL COIL

Another autumn of waiting
for the sky to clear of an old sorrow.

The stars are dead
that shimmer their elaborate reckoning.

Mother is gone

and not to China, or Pittsburgh, or Barneys
or heaven (though that would be quaint).

I'm 27, right-handed, thin & no one's.

## WHAT BECOMES A LEGEND MOST
ALTERNATIVES

Yesterday I had lunch with the man who would have been my father
had mother not left Laurinburg for men
no one back home would know.

This adolescent sweetheart is now a mechanic. He lives
in a beige house across the creek from the store that sold cat's eye
marbles mother used when she beat the boys at their games.

He remembers her winning streak & her skinny wrists. Asks if I recall
an August afternoon, the year after her death, when I, head newly shaved
passed four jeering rednecks outside Winn Dixie & paid them no mind?

All the time.

## ASSAULT ON A FIXED POSITION

I could have answered his questions,
fed & watered his ego but I didn't:
I wasn't playing for keeps.

Caught in the presence of an absence
he thought: *look no further* and I of hirsute
bottoms I couldn't revisit.

Perhaps a breeze or an ice cream truck melody
would saunter in & stay a while:
I left the porch door open as September.

## THE NATURAL WORLD DEFINED

Fluffed-up & in the mood for love
a pigeon struts, cooing.

It's 6 a.m.
the sun has caught me

askew again: home, elsewhere.

## LEGACY

Again in my apartment, showered, wearing the flannel plaid
pajamas my father gave me when I left for college
(him set & settled in his rest) I am left
with a sensation not unlike holding
a blunt & simple switchblade to the throat.

## THE SAFETY OF OBJECTS

Yesterday I cut the legs off the red
sock puppet I made for Mother's Day 1988

& stuffed those limbs
into the front pouch of my black bikini briefs.

It was cold out.
I wanted to make a good impression.

## UNDERSTUDY

I'm not late
No one's expecting me
Dinner when it comes will come prepackaged
Things are going according to plan
I'll be remembered as Rodney
Known for my way with the ladies
My thick ankles & commitment
To the truth

I can hardly wait
I'm in Union Square Park for now
Just west of the cow sculpture
Wearing a pastel-pink tank top
Brown cropped pants
(Reading *Paterson*)
Flocked by pigeons panhandlers
& happiness
Hurry

## DÉTENTE

Eventually we will be free of adjectives
and I will tell you of men who did not
survive past morning.

Of times morning-light caught me on the train
still dressed for darkness, my eyes
red-rimmed & skittish.

Eventually I will tell you everything
in a voice you may not recognize, a voice
born in backrooms, bars.

Soon we'll have had our fill of heroes
and be boys together & rest—bellies naked
to the voracious day.

## FATHER AFTER LONG SILENCE

I could no longer help me.

## BUDAPEST

It was not snowing. Above, chimneys:
charcoal streaks on a slack damask sky.

We crossed Szabadgag Bridge on foot
our bodies bundled, tame & not yet naked.

Behind & below a now-relenting winter;
ice, few birds, a chain of stumbling couples.

We (a coarse proficiency, a frangible
achievement) kept a decent distance.

## *HOPE IS A STRONG MAN'S ILLUSION*

I'm tired of lonely:
on the subway, outside the bodega

& in my room.
Too loudly it speaks to me;

if I answer, it will be in blood.
I should want to live, but my hands

shake & I cannot be convinced.
What are my chances?

## ANYMORE. JUST NOW. EVER.

I wanted to call & say:
it's 56° & raining,

yesterday, Jacob Waletsky
died (accidentally) of an overdose.

But that house has been empty
for thirteen years, come Wednesday

(mother is landlocked, an unbearable
roadside attraction)

and I need a little something
to take the edge off: for summer

finally to assert itself,
for the porch light to remain

on, the spare house-key hidden.

## MEMORY OF AN ISOLATED LOCATION

Whatever I have lost was not lost
        in this city of slow dusk & paper skyline.
I must look in other hemispheres.

        There must be a word of misdirection
*childhood* perhaps or *wallpaper*:
        brawn-brown & reminiscent

of razorblades & urgency
        in a basement bathroom: half-light,
quick cuts, an oval pattern.

## HOUSE AS BODY

She left in summer. Afterwards, the windows
refused to latch, the trashcans to contain

and my voice to thicken.
I did not think anything would change, ever—

Now, I try so very little: my hobbled heart
at the top of steep stairs.

## THE DIVISIBLE HEART

The last time I flew first class, Houston to Budapest via Paris
I looked out on what, at lower altitudes, would have been the Atlantic,

here cloud-backs & light. Recalled what mother had said
that day the Atlantic off Hatteras swallowed an old man,

returned him blue & stillborn to the beach:
*the ocean doesn't care*, she said. On that flight,

mother exactly eleven years dead, I knew
what she meant, she meant the world.

Rangi McNeil was born and raised in Laurinburg, North Carolina. He received a B.A. in History from Rice University in 1998. He is currently an MFA candidate at Columbia University's School of the Arts. He has lived in Houston, Prague and Budapest, and has worked for the Hungarian Parliament.